Writing Prompts For Boys

An A+ Teacher Design

By Christine Calabrese

Youtube Channel:
Mrs. Calabrese's Teaching Channel
https://www.youtube.com/c/MrsCalabresesTeachingChannel

For Antonio, Jordan, Jace and
all the boys I have taught.
You are my inspiration!

Other Books By Christine Calabrese

Little Pencil Finds His Forever Friends

Silly Little Scissors

Paper And Pencil Write A Story

Writing Prompts For Girls

A Note to Parents & Teachers:

These writing prompts are designed specifically to entice boys to write. Writing vocabulary supports the writing process. Sentence prompts along with punctuation and spelling tips are included. Creative sentence structure is addressed. Frequently used words are listed to assist with spelling. Tips for avoiding common writing blunders bolster confidence.

Advice:
Talk **before** writing! Use provided **vocabulary** to discuss topics and stimulate ideas for writing. To assist spelling and creativity, you may want to cut out and laminate the **Words You May Need** and **Replacement Words** pages for easy reference.
Include adjectives, adverbs, and prepositional phrases in composition; suggest the **Replacement Words** whenever possible.

Recommended Pencil Brands:
Koala Tools ~ Bear Claw Pencils or **Ticonderoga** pencils. **Music For Concentration Cd** by **Lawrence, Richard et al.**

Tip: Sharpen pencils **before** writing!
Safety Tip: Please remember to put your devices on **AIRPLANE MODE** after you download classical music.

Dear Boys,
Little Pencil hopes you enjoy this book.

Writing Advice:
Writing takes patience. Mistakes are common. Never give up! You can write!

Your Writing Area:
Before writing, put some classical music on your CD player or your computer.

Find a comfortable working space and make sure you have all your tools handy.

Writing Tools:
Pencils, Pencil Sharpener, Crayons, Colored Pencils, Markers, Classical Music. Optional: Dictionary, Thesaurus

Writing And Skyscrapers

Can you build a skyscraper?
Will you use paper or blocks?
The materials you choose will make a strong
building or a weak one, right?

Writing is like building.
The blocks are words.
The words create sentences
and the sentences make paragraphs.
Paragraphs make essays and stories.

Just like a builder chooses his materials
carefully to build a skyscraper, you must be
careful to choose interesting and creative
words when writing. There are some words
that kids use too much. This makes their
writing boring. Avoid these words when
writing:

*good, pretty, interesting, big, nice,
bad, ugly, mean, a lot*

Replacement Words:

good: admirable, brilliant, clever, delicious, fantastic, honorable, magnificent, powerful, respectable, supreme, terrific

pretty: beautiful, gorgeous, lovely, lush, majestic, stunning

interesting: amazing, captivating, exciting, fascinating, incredible, mysterious, puzzling

big: colossal, gigantic, huge, massive, monstrous, towering, vast

nice: charming, delightful, kind, pleasant, sweet

bad: corrupt, dishonest, evil, sinister, vicious, wicked

ugly: disgusting, grotesque, hideous, repulsive

mean: brutal, cold hearted, hardhearted, heartless, savage

a lot: countless, endless, innumerable, plenty, several, unlimited

This kid made some mistakes. What are they? How do you fix this?

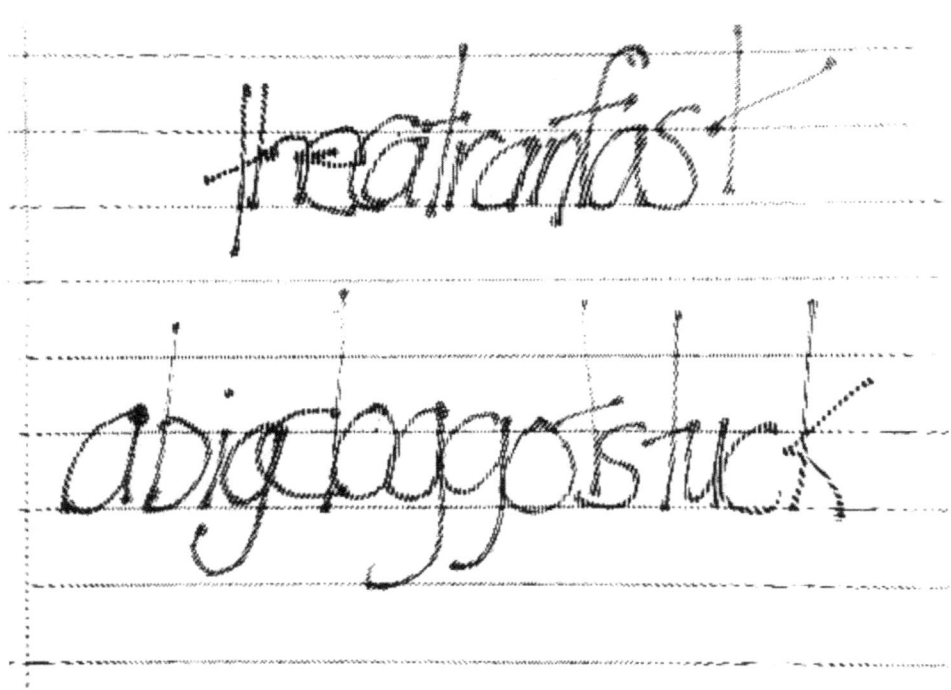

Note to parents: Say "Slide over" or use a pinky space or an index finger space to avoid this.

Fix those sentences!
Remember to add a capital and choose a
period, question mark or exclamation
mark to end the sentences. Spaces
between words are super important.

.!?   ?!.

Words You May Need:

a	down	is	other	to
about	each	it	out	two
all	find	its	part	up
am	first	like	people	use
an	for	long	said	was
and	from	look	see	water
are	get	made	she	way
as	go	make	so	we
at	had	many	some	were
be	has	may	than	what
been	had	more	that	when
but	he	my	the	which
by	her	no	their	who
call	him	not	them	will
can	his	now	then	with
come	how	number	there	word
could	I	of	these	would
day	if	on	they	write
did	in	one	this	you
do	into	your	time	your

More Words You May Need:

after	does	letter	over	such
again	end	line	page	take
air	even	little	picture	tell
also	farm	live	place	thing
America	follow	man	play	think

animal	found	me	point	three
another	give	mean	put	through
answer	good	men	read	too
any	great	most	right	try
around	hand	mother	same	turn

ask	help	move	say	us
away	here	much	sentence	very
back	home	must	said	want
because	house	name	should	well
before	just	need	show	went

big	kind	new	small	where
boy	know	off	snow	why
came	land	old	spell	work
change	large	only	still	world
different	learn	our	study	year

My Doodle Page. Listen to classical music, relax, draw, and just have fun!

1. Let's pretend you are captured by some bad guys and a superhero rescues you. Which superhero would you like to rescue you? Why? How? Where? When?

Writing
Vocabulary

Superman, Batman, Spiderman, Ironman, Thor, Captain America, free, brave, courageous, strong, scared, quickly, safe, running, mighty, power, punch, powerful, laser, hiding, under, behind, beneath, flying

Pick a sentence starter or write your own:

Yesterday I was grabbed...

Last night someone tugged...

This morning I was chased...

Draw a picture of the rescue.
Relax and color.
Tell someone about this drawing.

👀 Reflect on your drawing. ✏️
Write and describe: who, what,
where, when, why, how? Which
one? What kind? How many?

2. Some boys are really good at some things and not so good at other things. What are your best skills and your worst skills? Why? What will you do to improve? How?

Writing
Vocabulary

soccer, baseball, basketball, swimming, building, cars, running, climbing trees, math, times tables, reading, coloring, singing, drawing, speaking, writing, helping, cleaning, organizing, bike riding, sledding, snowball fights

Pick a sentence starter or write your own:

I am a fantastic... because...

One thing I need to improve on is...

If you challenge me in... you will find out that...

Draw a picture for this topic.
Relax and color.
Tell someone about this drawing.

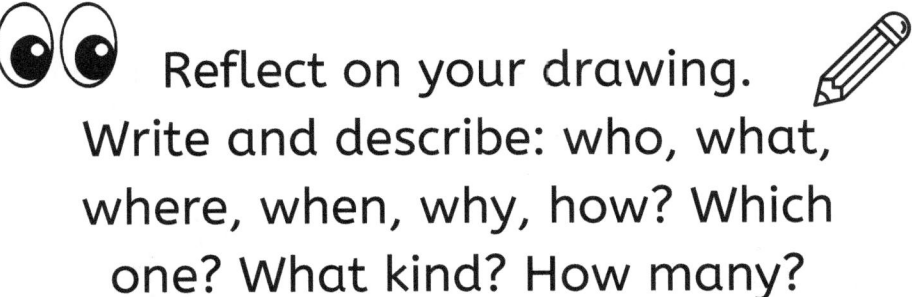 Reflect on your drawing.
Write and describe: who, what,
where, when, why, how? Which
one? What kind? How many?

3. If you could have any car or truck in the world, which one would you own? Why? Where would you take it? How fast would it go? What is special about this vehicle?

Writing

Vocabulary

pick-up truck, engine, race car, sports car, Corvette, SUV, fast, slow, quick, big, huge, tires, wheels, old, new, antique, future, electric, quiet, ride, steering wheel, racetrack

Pick a sentence starter or write your own:

I want a... because...

The racetrack is the best place for...

Traveling in a... is very comfortable because...

Draw a picture of your vehicle. Relax and color. Include the driver, passenger, and details.

Reflect on your drawing.
Write and describe: who, what,
where, when, why, how? Which
one? What kind? How many?

Spelling Tip:

Slow Motion the Word

1. Say the word VERY SLOWLY aloud.

2. Listen for letter sounds as you say the word.

3. Write down all the sounds you hear in the word.

4. Do not worry about spelling exactly right.

5. Your teacher will help you correct it later.

Note to Instructors:
This is called "**inventive**" or "**invented**" spelling. This works best if your student has a good working knowledge of letter sounds. Allow children to write what they hear, then check it and have them rewrite the words properly.

Tip: Often we have to ask our students to read their work to us because the words are not discernible.

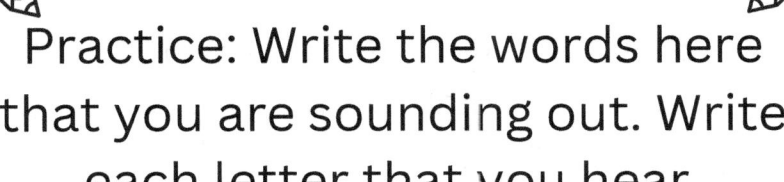

Practice: Write the words here that you are sounding out. Write each letter that you hear.

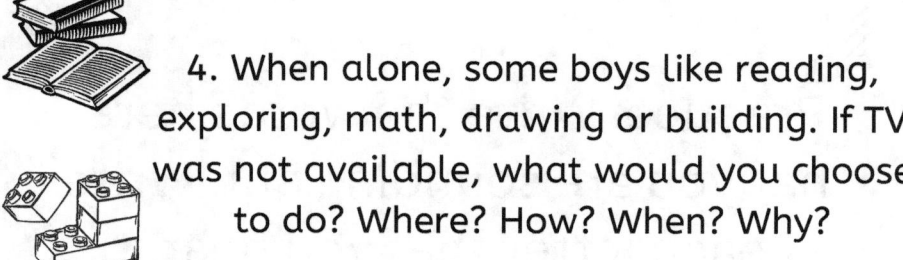

4. When alone, some boys like reading, exploring, math, drawing or building. If TV was not available, what would you choose to do? Where? How? When? Why?

Writing
Vocabulary

walking the dog, horses, chickens, practicing, guitar, drums, building, Legos, coloring, drawing, writing, practicing, nature walks, woods, gardening, bike riding, exploring, creating, cooking, reading

Pick a sentence starter or write your own:

When I am finally alone, I like to...

It's hard to decide what to do because...

On a quiet day, my favorite activities include...

Draw a picture of you and your favorite alone time.
Relax and color.
Tell someone about this drawing.

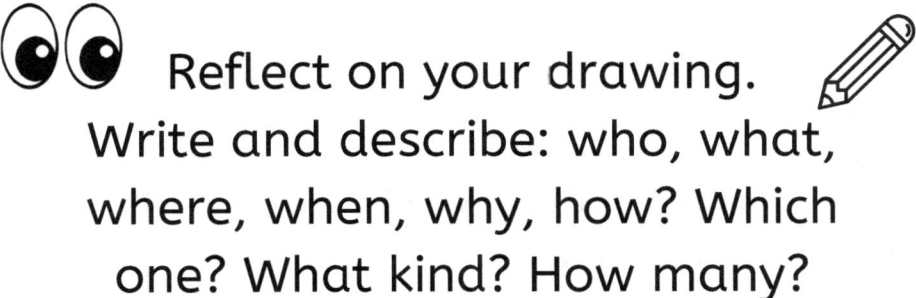

Reflect on your drawing.
Write and describe: who, what, where, when, why, how? Which one? What kind? How many?

5. Let's pretend you are king of a castle. Suddenly, your castle is attacked. Where is your castle? Who is attacking? Why? How will you save your castle? Who will help you?

Writing Vocabulary

suddenly, enemy, treasure, thieves, stole, stolen, queen, princess, gold, crown, dungeon, snakes, throne, silver, safe, horses, riding, knights, night, ran, sword, shield, children

Pick a sentence starter or write your own:

While I was taking my morning ride...

I called to my best knights, "Come! Quickly!" and...

The queen yelled for help, and I ran to...

Draw a picture of this story. Add details.
Try using colored pencils.

Reflect on your drawing.
Write and describe: who, what,
where, when, why, how? Which
one? What kind? How many?

6. In the Wild West danger lurked everywhere. Pretend you are a cowboy chasing bandits who stole your cattle. Will you catch them and retrieve your cattle? How? Where? When?

Writing Vocabulary

lasso, range, horses, guns, rifle, arrow, shot, gallop, hiding, scared, rear, fell, bushes, cash, bank, robber, robbing, dogs, cattle, bounty, saloon, cows, calves, sheriff

Pick a sentence starter or write your own:

A shot rang out and suddenly...

I jumped on my horse and...

I smashed into the saloon and found the...

Draw a picture of the chase.
Relax and color.

Reflect on your drawing.
Write and describe: who, what,
where, when, why, how? Which
one? What kind? How many?

7. Most boys love a snowstorm. What are your favorite activities when it snows? Why? Where? Who do you play in the snow?

Writing
Vocabulary

fort, snowball fight, ice ball, wet, snow boots, snow pants, snowman, carrots, rocks, sticks, fluffy, slide, ice skate, sledding, snow fort, slide, hills, down, fall, snow angel, hot chocolate, marshmallows

Pick a sentence starter or write your own:

Making a snow fort is...

The biggest snowman I ever made was...

We went sleigh riding down a huge hill...

Draw a picture of your snowy day fun.

Reflect on your drawing.
Write and describe: who, what,
where, when, why, how? Which
one? What kind? How many?

Listen to classical music. Draw anything.

👀 Reflect on your drawing. ✏️
Write and describe: who, what,
where, when, why, how? Which
one? What kind? How many?

Enhance The Sentence
Remember!

A sentence creates a picture in your mind. We can practice by starting with a simple sentence and adding details.

Read and imagine each sentence.

- A flag waved.

- A beautiful flag waved.

- A beautiful, American flag waved.

- A beautiful, American flag waved above the house.

- A new, beautiful, American flag waved above the house.

Talk about how the picture in your mind changed as the sentences changed. Why did it change?

Now You Try it!

Words to help: crazy, tiny, funny, joyful, kind, quickly, speedily ~ on the couch, up the hill, off the chair

1. The cat jumped.

2.

3.

4.

5.

Talk about how the picture in your mind changed as the sentences changed. Why did it change?

8. What is your favorite sport? Why? Where do you play? Who do you play with? What position do you play? Why?

Writing
Vocabulary

football, soccer, baseball, tennis, volleyball, basketball, racing, running, dodgeball, handball, racquetball, swimming, win, lose, challenge, chess, board games, monopoly

Pick a sentence starter or write your own:

My favorite sport is... because...

Don't challenge me in... you'll lose because...

I do not like sports, but I do like...

Draw a detailed picture of your favorite sport.

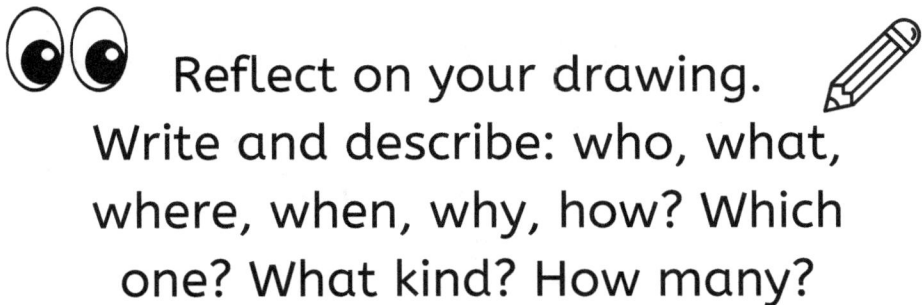

Reflect on your drawing.
Write and describe: who, what,
where, when, why, how? Which
one? What kind? How many?

Some kids made mistakes with
end marks, capitals and spacing.
? Fix these sentences. **!**

●

1. thecatjumped?

2. dogs bark too much.

3. what will youhave.

4. stop that

5. run fast tothe house?

Think About It:

Did you know that the first sentence
in a story is called the "hook."
A "hook" is a sentence that makes the
reader want to continue reading.
A question makes a reader curious.
Asking a question can make a good hook.

Here are some examples of story
starters
that are questions.

1.   Have you ever seen a dragon?
2. Did you know that snakes sleep a lot?
3.   Are you great at soccer?
4.   Can you drive a hot rod?
5.   Have you ever had a banana split?

Try starting your writing with a
question and see if you think it hooks
your readers.

 9. Imagine that you are a knight. A treasure chest has been stolen and the king wants you to find it. How, where, and when will you find it? How will the king reward you?

Writing Vocabulary

shield, armor, princess, prince, warrior, thief, thieves, fight, sword, horse, swing, save, dragon, fire, flying, gallop, find, gold, treasure, silver, armor

Pick a sentence starter or write your own:

A two-headed dragon...

The princess stole the treasure because...

A servant in the castle told me where...

Draw a picture of a knight.
Can you add interesting
details to your drawing?
Relax and color.

Reflect on your drawing.
Write and describe: who, what, where, when, why, how? Which one? What kind? How many?

Draw a picture of the treasure chest or your reward.

Reflect on your drawing. Write and describe: who, what, where, when, why, how? Which one? What kind? How many?

10. What would you like for dinner? Dessert? Who will make it? Why? How? Where will you eat and with whom?

Writing
Vocabulary

steak, hamburgers, pizza, lasagna, chicken, spaghetti, beans, rice, turkey, potatoes, pie, ice cream, chocolate cake, restaurant, mom, dad, grandma, grandpa, French fries, fried, broccoli, carrots, peas, corn on the cob

Pick a sentence starter or write your own:

My favorite food is... because...

The best cook I know is... because...

There's a restaurant that serves...

Draw a detailed picture of your favorite meal.

Reflect on your drawing.
Write and describe: who, what,
where, when, why, how? Which
one? What kind? How many?

Spelling Game!

Materials: Rubber Band, Word List

1. Imagine a word you cannot spell is on a rubber band,
stretch it out and listen for the sounds.

2. Use the next page to write down all the sounds you hear in the word.

3. You get a point for every letter you get right.

4. Lose a point for an incorrect letter.

Suggested Points: 20 points and you win but if you lose 10 points your opponent wins!

Note to Instructors:
Try spelling the words provided in "**Words You May Need**."
Demonstrate by saying a word fast then slowly as you stretch a rubber band. Try taping a word to the relaxed rubber band and then stretch it!
Watch and listen with your student.

Write the words you are sounding out here.

Enhance The Sentence
Examples:

A sentence creates a picture in your mind. As a writer you get to illustrate this picture with words.

Read and imagine each sentence.

A dragon flew.

A huge dragon flew.

A green, huge dragon flew slowly.

The green, huge dragon flew slowly over the mountains.

Think: At first, we can imagine a dragon. Next, with new words we can imagine **what kind** of dragon. Finally, we imagine **how** he flew and **where** he flew.

Enhance The Sentences

Suggested Words: wild, black, young, happily, high, sneaky

1. The mouse jumped.

Suggested Words: three, two, quietly, loudly, in the park

2. The kids played.

Suggested Words: small, big, high, fast, up the wall, in the tree

3. The boys climbed.

Suggested Words: little, fat, loudly, quietly, in the church, in his crib

4. The baby cried.

11. Let's pretend you are captain of a huge ship. You spot pirates approaching. How will you defeat these enemy pirates? Who will help you?

Writing
Vocabulary

Blackbeard, sword, arrows, cannons, wind, race, hide, treasure, mate, shipmate, capture, on board, men, children, women, ransom, chest, afraid, weather, rifle, gun, chased, sail

Pick a sentence starter or write your own:

Have you ever been really scared?

As the pirate ship approached, I ordered...

Thankfully the wind picked up and we...

Draw a picture of your pirate attack. Add details.

👀 Reflect on your drawing. ✏️
Write and describe: who, what,
where, when, why, how? Which
one? What kind? How many?

12. Imagine that you go into a secret room in your house, and you open a door that leads to another world. What do you find? Who are you with? Where do you think you are? Can you get back safely?

Writing Vocabulary

suddenly, gold, treasure, secret, passage, key, yell, help, friend, rescue, box, desk, window, knock, escape, dark, light, cold, warm, hiding, magic, forest, winter, summer, trees, talking

Pick a sentence starter or write your own:

Have you ever been to...?

I knew I shouldn't have gone into that room but...

If there was a secret room, I'd probably find...

Draw a detailed picture of
the secret room.

👀 Reflect on your drawing. ✏️
Write and describe: who, what,
where, when, why, how? Which
one? What kind? How many?

13. Let's pretend you have a flying carpet that can take you anywhere. Where would you go? Why? What would you see? Who would you take with you?

Writing
Vocabulary

fly, moon, planet, country, states, countries, stars, aliens, ships, purple, blue, orange, huge, tiny, friends, playground, candy land, chocolate factory

Pick a sentence starter or write your own:

Have you ever been to the moon?

"Fly!" I commanded my carpet and...

Once I saw the most beautiful star...

Draw a detailed picture of your trip.

Reflect on your drawing.
Write and describe: who, what, where, when, why, how? Which one? What kind? How many?

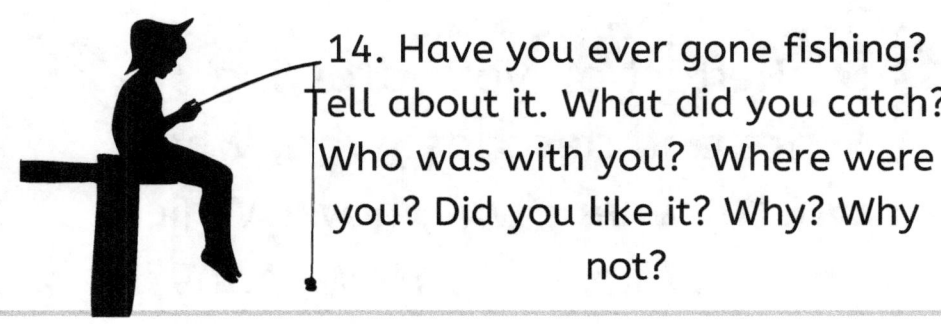

14. Have you ever gone fishing? Tell about it. What did you catch? Who was with you? Where were you? Did you like it? Why? Why not?

Writing
Vocabulary

boat, dock, family, friends, dad, waves, wait, morning, night, evening, mom, sister, bass, gigantic, tiny, net, beach, pier, swimming, father, sailboat, strong, swordfish, bait, hook, fishing rod

Pick a sentence starter or write your own:

Do you know how to catch a fish?
Once I caught a...
I've never been fishing but if I could go I would...

Draw a detailed picture of your day of fishing.

Reflect on your drawing.
Write and describe: who, what, where, when, why, how? Which one? What kind? How many?

15. Let's pretend you discover a cave, and you explore it. What do you find? Is it dark or light? Why? Is there treasure? Are there any animals? Are they dangerous?

Writing Vocabulary

bats, bear, snakes, scared,
crystals, spring, waterfalls,
echo, deep, old, dirt, spiders,
webs, fossils, dinosaur,
treasure, gold, silver, cold,
ice, colorful, water, air,
breathing, dragon

Pick a sentence starter or write your own:

Did you ever go into a dark cave in the forest?
Once I was in a cave and I saw...

Deep in a cave I found fossils which looked like...

Draw a detailed picture of the cave.

Reflect on your drawing. Write and describe: who, what, where, when, why, how? Which one? What kind? How many?

16. Most boys like to camp in the woods. Have you ever gone camping? Where? What was the best and worst of it? Why?

Writing Vocabulary

quiet, books, bugs, mosquitoes, bats, bears, snakes, spiders, webs, fire, marshmallows, s'mores, smell, tent, sleeping bag, water, drinks, scream, owl, hot dogs, hamburgers

Pick a sentence starter or write your own:

What would you do if you heard... camping?

The best time I had camping was...

Even though I've never been camping I think I'd like...

Draw a detailed picture of your camping experience.

Reflect on your drawing.
Write and describe: who, what, where, when, why, how? Which one? What kind? How many?

17. If you were in a contest to build the best sandcastle, what would it look like? How would you build it? What tools would you need? How big would it be?

Writing Vocabulary

dig, water, shovel, bucket, friends, sand, hole, tower, high, cups, mold, shells, waves

Pick a sentence starter or write your own:

Have you ever built a sandcastle?

The best sandcastles are...

I do not like contests but when I build sandcastles I...

Draw a detailed picture of your sandcastle.

Reflect on your drawing. Write and describe: who, what, where, when, why, how? Which one? What kind? How many?

18. Climbing trees is an adventure! Write about a time you climbed a tree. What did you see? How high were you? Where were you?

Writing Vocabulary

branches, twigs, nest, bird, squirrel, bugs, far, near, hiding, under, above, scary, easy, hard, oak, pine, heights, afraid, tree house

Pick a sentence starter or write your own:

What can you see from a tree?

Once I climbed a big tree and...

I do not like to climb trees because...

Draw a detailed picture of your tree climbing adventure.

Reflect on your drawing.
Write and describe: who, what,
where, when, why, how? Which
one? What kind? How many?

19. Where is your favorite playground? What is your favorite thing to do there? Why? Who do you play with? When? How do you get there?

Writing Vocabulary

swings, slides, climb, monkey bars, handles, chase, hide, pretend, play, friends, bike, drive, car, mom, dad

Pick a sentence starter or write your own:

Can you complete the monkey bars?

My favorite playground is... because...

I cannot pick a favorite playground because...

Draw a detailed picture of the playground.

Reflect on your drawing.
Write and describe: who, what, where, when, why, how? Which one? What kind? How many?

 20. Can you fix things? What is the hardest thing you ever fixed? Who helped you? Where were you? What tools did you use? In your opinion, what is the easiest thing to fix?

Writing Vocabulary

broken, lamp, toolbox, saw, jack, knife, scissors, Philips head screwdriver, hammer, wrench, screwdriver, nails, screws, house, home, oil

Pick a sentence starter or write your own:

Can you fix a...?

The hardest thing to fix is... because...

I do not like to fix anything because...

Draw a detailed picture of something you fixed or broke.

Reflect on your drawing.
Write and describe: who, what, where, when, why, how? Which one? What kind? How many?

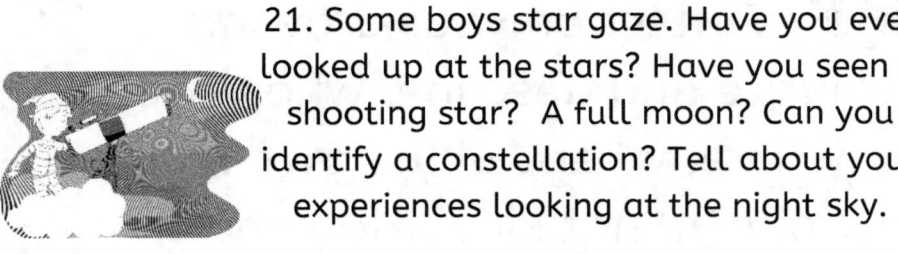

21. Some boys star gaze. Have you ever looked up at the stars? Have you seen a shooting star? A full moon? Can you identify a constellation? Tell about your experiences looking at the night sky.

Writing Vocabulary

bed, early, constellations, Mercury, Venus, Mars, moon, telescope, crescent, half, black, bright, cold, night, late, big dipper, hot chocolate, marshmallows

Pick a sentence starter or write your own:

Have you ever seen a shooting star?

I love a starry night because...

I have not seen many starry nights because...

Draw a detailed picture of a a night sky.

Reflect on your drawing.
Write and describe: who, what,
where, when, why, how? Which
one? What kind? How many?

22. Have you been to an amusement or theme park? Which one? Where? Who takes you? What is your favorite ride? Is there a ride you do not like? Why?

Writing Vocabulary

ferris wheel, roller coaster, haunted house, bumper cars, teacup rides, swings, water slides, water park, bathing suit, slippery, high

Pick a sentence starter or write your own:

Have you ever been on a roller coaster?

The best ride I have ever been on is...

I had a bad experience at the... because...

Draw a detailed picture of the park.

Reflect on your drawing.
Write and describe: who, what,
where, when, why, how? Which
one? What kind? How many?

23. Sometimes Dad needs help with chores. What do you like to help your dad doing? Is it outside or inside? When do you do this chore? Tell about the chores you do with your father.

Writing Vocabulary

garage, car, basement, tools, tires, car wash, fixing, roof, motor, grilling, move, lifting, chop wood, hammer, nails, screws, building, design, cleaning, sweeping

Pick a sentence starter or write your own:

Does your dad let you help him?

Together, my dad and I enjoy...

One time I helped my father with the...

Draw a detailed picture of the you and your father doing a chore.

Reflect on your drawing.
Write and describe: who, what,
where, when, why, how? Which
one? What kind? How many?

The Writing Journey
by Christine Calabrese

Writing takes time,
And practice too,
With words in phrases,
And grammar to do.

There's lots to learn,
Challenging you.
A difficult task,
In something new.

But you can do this,
Oh yes you can!
I'm one hundred percent,
Your greatest fan.

Most Sincerely,
Mrs. Calabrese

www.ingramcontent.com/pod-product-compliance
Lightning Source LLC
Chambersburg PA
CBHW071203120626
46546CB00006B/2393